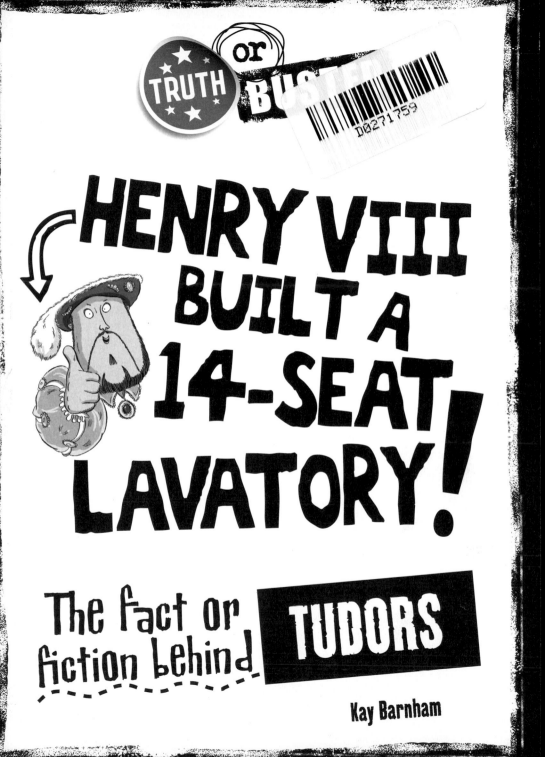

TRUTH or BUSTED

D0271759

HENRY VIII BUILT A 14-SEAT LAVATORY!

The fact or fiction behind **TUDORS**

Kay Barnham

WAYLAND

First published in 2014 by Wayland

Copyright © Wayland 201

Wayland
338 Euston Road
London NW1 3BH

Wayland Australia
Level 17/207 Kent Street
Sydney, NSW 2000

Editor: Elizabeth Brent
Design: Rocket Design (East Anglia) Ltd
Illustration: Alex Paterson

A catalogue record for this book is available from the British Library.
ISBN: 978 0 7502 8130 0
eBook ISBN: 978 0 7502 8729 6
Dewey Number: 942'.05-dc23

Printed in China
10 9 8 7 6 5 4 3 2 1

Wayland is a division of Hachette Children's Books,
an Hachette UK company
www.hachette.co.uk

All illustrations by Shutterstock, except 4, 7, 20–21, 33, 43, 48–49, 54–55, 63, 66, 71, 74–75, 83, 88–89. Illustration on p10 by Alan Irvine.

read on!

Read this bit first...!

Who *were* the Tudors?

Easy. They were the monarchs who belonged to the massively powerful House of Tudor — the royal family that ruled England and Ireland between 1485 and 1603.

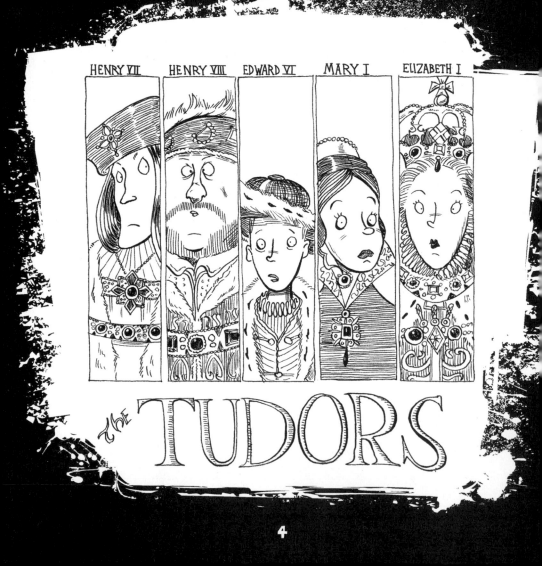

HENRY VII   HENRY VIII   EDWARD VI   MARY I   ELIZABETH I

The TUDORS

Henry Tudor came first. He famously beat Richard III at the Battle of Bosworth to become Henry VII. Next up was his son, Henry VIII, who is best known for his nasty habit of chopping off his wives' heads. (And quite a lot of other heads too.) Then, in quick succession, Henry VIII's children followed him onto the throne: Edward VI (king for just six years), Mary I (queen for a mere five years) and, finally, Elizabeth I (who was quite possibly the most splendid of them all).

But there were other Tudors too, because EVERYONE who lived under Tudor rule was known as a Tudor. Most of these Tudors weren't even a little bit royal and didn't eat swan for their dinner or wear fancy clothes woven with gold or have someone to wipe their bottom for them.
Instead, life could be very tough indeed.

(All totally true facts!)

Read on to find out what it was really like being a Tudor, rich OR poor. And find out which of the following silly statements is true...

⭐ *Tudor cooks baked live birds inside pies!*

⭐ *Henry VIII ordered 500 people to be beheaded!*

⭐ *Plague doctors soaked their clothes in Thai fish sauce!*

Made your mind up? Great! Now you can read the rest of this book to see if you were right or not. But be prepared. You're about to bust the myths and find out the truth about one of the most exciting — and dangerous — periods of history. Whatever you do, don't lose your head (like Anne Boleyn).

read on!

Henry VII was mean and miserly

In August 1485, Henry Tudor ended the Wars of the Roses by defeating Richard III* at the Battle of Bosworth. As Henry VII, he officially kicked off the Tudor dynasty. But once he was on the throne, it's said that Henry was mean with his money. So WAS he an old miser...?

★ And the truth is...

Henry VII didn't exactly throw money around, but he certainly wasn't as tight-fisted as some say.

Some barons had caused him an awful lot of bother during the Wars of the Roses by renting out their private armies to both sides. So the king got his own back afterwards by taxing them HEAVILY and using the money to build up his royal army instead. He certainly knew how to make money work for him, which perhaps earned him a reputation for being mean.

But Henry VII knew how to enjoy himself too. He liked to play cards and one evening gambled away the same amount of money that a farm worker earned IN AN ENTIRE YEAR.

Verdict:  BUSTED

ZOUNDS!

Henry VII showed that he wasn't a skinflint on his wedding day, by forking out for Britain's very first firework display.

*The remains of poor Richard III were discovered under a car park in Leicester in the UK in 2012, where he'd lain for more than 500 years.

Henry VIII was larger than life

Henry VIII was a hugely important figure in the history of England, and in many paintings he *looks* huge too. But was he really THAT big in real life?

★ And the truth is...

In his twenties, Henry VIII was super fit, muscly and at least 6 feet 1 inch (185cm), and possibly as much as 6 feet 3 inches (just over 190cm), tall too. He was definitely not overweight. When historians checked his armour, they found that the young king's waistline measured a trim 32 inches (81cm) and his chest 39 (99cm) inches, making him a fine figure of a man. So did he stay that way?

Er, no.

By his late forties, Henry measured 48 inches (121cm) around the middle. And by the end of his reign, the Tudor king had a whopping 52-inch (132cm) waist and a 53-inch (134cm) chest.

Verdict:  but not until later in life.

8

> # Edward VI was only nine years old when he became king of England

Nine years old? No way. Even if Edward was as bright as historians say — he could speak fluent Greek AND Latin, for example — surely nine is FAR too young to be king?

 And the truth is...

Not a bit of it. Because Edward was only nine years old when his father Henry VIII died, that was the age he became king. He didn't actually rule the country though. That was the job of powerful nobles like the Duke of Somerset and the Duke of Northumberland, who ruled on the boy's behalf (as well as arguing among themselves over who should be in charge). But as his health grew steadily worse, it became clear that he was never going to grow old enough to be a proper king and poor Edward died when he was just 16 years old.

Verdict: _____

Henry VIII built a 14-seat lavatory

Well, he *was* the king, which meant that Henry VIII could do whatever he liked. And if he fancied building a 14-seat lavatory for himself and 13 close friends, then why not?

⭐ And the truth is...

Actually, the massive toilet that was built at Hampton Court Palace for Henry VIII didn't have 14 seats. It had 28. Known as the common jakes, there were four rows of loos, with seven seats apiece.

So Henry VIII must have loved spending time in the common jakes, chatting with his friends and courtiers, right?

Not a bit of it.

Henry — who spent quite a lot of time on the toilet, due to a very meaty diet that gave him terrible constipation — had his own lavatory. It was called a closed stool. This was simply a fancy box with a chamber pot hidden inside. On top was a sumptuous padded seat, for the king to park his bottom on.

Verdict:  BUSTED

ZOUNDS!

Don't worry about the king being lonely while he was on the toilet though. He did have company. That was the groom of the stool. What was his job? To wipe the king's bottom, of course. Well, you couldn't expect a KING to do it.

TUDOR TITBITS

I kid you not!

It didn't matter if a Tudor monarch was at death's door – no doctor with any sense would tell them that they were dying. This was because the Treason Act forbade ANYONE to predict, or even speak of, a monarch's death.

The punishment? Death, obviously.

So when Henry VIII was on his deathbed on 28 January 1547, aged 56, no one said a word... Or else.

Pssst! He died anyway, of course. Not speaking of the king's death didn't mean that it wasn't going to happen.

Henry VIII invented a brand new church

Er, is that even allowed?

⭐ **And the truth is...**

The Roman Catholic Church certainly didn't think so.

But when Henry VIII became bored of being married to Catherine of Aragon (who failed to give him a son and heir) and wanted to marry Anne Boleyn instead (who he hoped WOULD give birth to a boy) he decided that it was his only option. If the Pope would not allow him to get a divorce, he would simply start a new Protestant church — one that *would* allow him to remarry. He called his brand new church the Church of England. And one divorce and one marriage later, he had a brand new queen too.

Verdict:

Mary I was nicknamed Bloody Mary because she had so many people executed

When the Roman Catholic Church refused to let Henry VIII divorce his first wife, Catherine of Aragon (Mary I's mother), the resourceful king simply changed his country's religion to Protestant and *then* divorced Catherine.

Later, when his son Edward VI became king, he burned anyone at the stake who refused to become Protestant. This horrified his half-sister Mary, who had been brought up Roman Catholic.

★ And the truth is...

Mary I *did* order 287 Protestants to be burned at the stake during her reign. Her treatment of them made her very unpopular, earning her the nickname Bloody Mary. But she was nowhere near as bloodthirsty as her father. It's thought that Henry VIII sent as many as 57,000 people to their deaths while he was king. No one is sure of the exact number. Maybe they just lost count.

Verdict: TRUTH — but she wasn't as bad as her dad

Anne Boleyn had an extra finger

Henry VIII's second wife had a lot of enemies. But did she really have a lot of fingers too?

★ And the truth is...

Nicholas Sanders was a Roman Catholic priest living abroad. And he thought that Catherine of Aragon should be queen, NOT Anne Boleyn. So he tried to blacken the new queen's name by telling everyone that she'd used witchcraft to make Henry VIII marry her. Soon everyone was gossiping about Anne. She had six fingers on one hand, they said. And sticky-out teeth. And what about that massive mole under her chin? That totally proved she was a witch, they said.

But the gossip should be taken with a pinch of salt. Perhaps Anne did have buck teeth and a mole. Maybe she did have a growth on her hand. But if so, it must have been VERY, VERY tiny, because Henry would not have chased her for so long and made so many enemies, to put someone on the throne who risked being called a witch.

Verdict: Almost certainly **BUSTED** but so what if it isn't? After all, nobody's perfect

15

Henry VIII killed his wife with kindness

Unfortunately, Anne Boleyn didn't bear Henry VIII the boy he longed for. She did have a daughter — who later became Elizabeth I, one of the greatest queens EVER — but that was no use to Henry who was desperate for a son and heir. So Anne Boleyn's days were numbered, especially as Henry now had his eye on another lady at court called Jane Seymour.

By not-so-very-huge coincidence, Anne was accused of seeing other men, then tried and found guilty on the flimsiest of evidence. The punishment for this crime was death.

So what's kind about that?

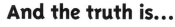 **And the truth is...**

Even though Henry VIII was putting his own wife to death, he had a choice about how to do it. He could have Anne Boleyn burned at the stake (a slow, painful and grisly death) or have her beheaded instead (a much faster dispatching). Kind-hearted Henry opted for a swift beheading, so Anne wouldn't suffer too much.

What a thoroughly, um, nice chap.

But Henry VIII went even further. He could have had the queen's head chopped off with an axe, but it sometimes took a few blows to finish someone off and was, presumably, quite painful. So instead, the king went to the trouble and expense of hiring an expert French swordsman to do the deed. And when Anne Boleyn knelt on the scaffold at the Tower of London on 19 May 1536, her head was taken off in one clean stroke.

Lucky old Anne.

though he did sentence her to death in the first place, which wasn't THAT kind

Verdict:  TRUTH

Henry VIII's third wife could barely read or write

Jane Seymour was born in either 1508 or 1509. (No one is exactly sure.) Henry VIII didn't waste time after Anne Boleyn's execution, marrying Jane just 11 days afterwards. So was the new queen a well-educated young woman?

★ And the truth is...

Not really. When she married the king, the only thing Jane Seymour could read and write was her own name. But this was hardly her fault. In Tudor times, it was virtually unheard of for girls to receive any sort of formal education. However, she was pretty good at needlework and household management. And she did give Henry VIII what he dearly wanted — a son, Edward. Sadly, Jane died from blood poisoning just 12 days after the baby's birth.

Awwww.

Verdict:  TRUTH

TUDOR TITBITS

I kid you not!

Anne of Cleves was the fourth of Henry VIII's wives and one of the most fortunate of the lot. She wasn't beheaded, for starters. And she didn't die after childbirth. She was divorced by the king instead AND given several properties and money in the settlement.

Lucky escape!

P.S. Don't believe what they say about her looking like a horse. True, Anne of Cleves' smallpox scars were not included in the portrait Henry VIII commissioned when he was deciding whether to marry her or not, and it's said that he flinched when he met her in true life (what a gent!). But their split is much more likely to be because they just didn't get on.

Tudors weren't allowed to parp at the dinner table

Ha ha ha ha ha ha!

How funny!

Er... that's a joke, right?

⭐ And the truth is...

The average Tudor could do whatever they liked at their own dinner table, but if you were one of Henry VIII's courtiers at Eltham Palace, then trouser trumpeting was SERIOUSLY frowned upon. Burping at the dinner table? That was banned too.

However, the rules didn't say anything about whether Tudors were allowed to burp or trump elsewhere, so perhaps they could just go and be windy in a wardrobe instead.

Verdict:

if the table was a royal one

Here are five more totally true rules from Eltham Palace:

1. No one is allowed to have greyhounds or other dogs at court, except for ladies, who can bring a small spaniel or two. *(That's rough. Ruff? RUFF?! Oh, never mind.)*

2. No person can bring to court more servants than his position in society allows. *(In other words, you can't have more servants than the king.)*

3. Kitchen boys cannot go naked or wear scruffy clothing; nor can they sleep in the kitchen by the fireside at night. *(So it isn't a terribly good place to be Cinderella.)*

4. The only people permitted in the king's bedroom are the Marquis of Exeter, six waiters, two ushers, four grooms, the barber and the page. *(And the groom of the stool, of course. See page 11.)*

5. Courtiers cannot fight or kill anyone within the court. Failure to observe this rule means a trip to the Fleet Prison.

Catherine Parr's body stayed fresh for 234 years

Catherine Parr was the last of Henry VIII's six wives, whom he married in 1543. She'd been married twice before her wedding to the king and after his death in 1547, she married a fourth time. (To this day, she holds the record for being The English Queen Who Married More Times Than Any Other. She was also The First English Queen To Have A Book Published Under Her Own Name. Go, Catherine!)

The following year, she gave birth to a daughter — Lady Mary Seymour — but died only six days later.

So how *did* she stay fresh for the next 234 years?

★ And the truth is...

Catherine was buried at Sudeley Castle, in Gloucestershire, UK, which later fell into ruins. Then, in 1782, a man called John Locust discovered Catherine's coffin in the remains of Sudeley Castle chapel. He opened the coffin and — *ta daaaa!* — found that the old queen's body was still in tip top condition.

Or so he said.

Locust claimed that the flesh on one of Catherine's arms was still white and moist. And before he sealed the coffin again, he took a few locks of her hair. (Nice.)

Ten years later, her coffin was opened once more, then reburied UPSIDE DOWN. And when the coffin was officially reopened in 1817, nothing but a skeleton remained.

Now, FINALLY, Catherine Parr is resting in peace.

Verdict: Oh, come on. REALLY?

BUSTED

Catherine Howard two-timed the king

By 1540, Henry VIII had become very overweight. He was 49 and suffered from open ulcers on his leg. And he'd just divorced Anne of Cleves and needed someone who could cheer him up. That someone was Catherine Howard — the previous queen's maid of honour. She was said to be a bright, cheerful soul and the perfect person to make the king happy. Henry thought she was FABULOUS and called her his 'rose without a thorn'.

No one is exactly sure when Catherine was born, but she was probably just a teenager when she married Henry VIII.

Why did she marry someone so much older than herself?

Simply, because she didn't really have a choice. It wasn't the done thing to disobey the king and especially not one who lost his head — and other people's — as often as Henry VIII.

So would she REALLY have risked having other boyfriends at the same time as being married to the king?

★ And the truth is...

Like her cousin Anne Boleyn — Henry's second wife — Catherine Howard had MANY enemies. They wanted to get rid of her. And to do this, they had to gather enough evidence of Catherine's wrongdoings to present to the king. Because by now, EVERYONE knew what happened to people who did anything to upset Henry VIII.

Catherine did have other boyfriends before the royal wedding, but it's not known if she went out with other people afterwards. Nevertheless, two old flames — Thomas Culpeper and Frances Dareham — were arrested, condemned, tortured and beheaded. Their heads were stuck on London Bridge.

As for Catherine, she was stripped of her title of queen, imprisoned and beheaded on 13 February 1542. She was probably no older than 20.

Verdict: **TRUST** and **BUSTED**

but who cares?
She didn't deserve to lose her head over it!

Elizabeth I was killed by her make-up

Was she murdered by her mascara?

Beheaded by her blusher?

Whodunnit?!

⭐ And the truth is...

At the age of 28, a nasty bout of smallpox left Elizabeth I with pockmarked skin. But this wasn't a problem for the queen. She just covered the scars with thick, white make-up, which was very fashionable at the time. (Now? Not so much.) Elizabeth also suffered from hair loss, which she hid under a huge variety of wigs. As for her rotten, black teeth, she simply closed her mouth when artists were painting her. She needn't have bothered though, because official portraits were only allowed to show the queen at her very best. In fact, to make it easier for everyone, she had templates made of how she wanted to look and artists simply copied those.

So what about the dastardly make-up...?

The thing is that Elizabeth's white make-up — ceruse, which was a mixture of white lead and vinegar — was VERY POISONOUS. And it may be that this make-up slowly killed her.

So it wasn't the mascara or the blusher whodunnit. Elizabeth I was finished off by face paint.

Verdict: ⭐TRUTH⭐ probably

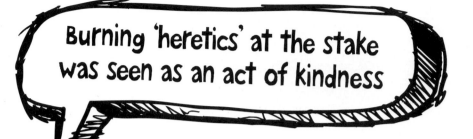

Burning 'heretics' at the stake was seen as an act of kindness

Religion was VERY important in Tudor times. If you didn't follow the same faith as your ruler then you were in serious danger of being called a 'heretic' — someone who didn't believe. And this was something you REALLY didn't want to happen to you. Heretics were sentenced to death by burning at the stake, which was a punishment meant to symbolise the flames that awaited the sinner in hell. Although used throughout the Tudor period, this punishment reached a peak during the reign of Mary I.*

Paintings from Tudor times show heretics standing in a tar barrel at the stake. Bundles of wood, called faggots, were heaped around them. And if the victims were lucky, they were given opium to deaden the pain. Sometimes relatives even managed to tie a bag of gunpowder around the victim's neck to finish them off more quickly. And occasionally the heretic would be strangled before the faggots were lit.

So how is this supposed to be an act of kindness exactly?

*See page 14.

⭐ And the truth is...

Incredible as it may seem, burning at the stake was thought to purify the body and allow the soul a safe passage to heaven.

Er... right.

Verdict:  except it clearly wasn't

TUDOR RASCALS

SIR PHILIP SIDNEY, THE TOP TUDOR POET (1554-86)

Sir Philip Sidney was a celebrity poet who lived during the reign of Elizabeth I. But he didn't just write poetry, he was a courtier too, which meant that he got to carry out **Very Important Tasks** for the queen.

So, in 1572, Elizabeth I sent him to France to discuss her possible marriage to the Duke of Anjou. And even though she was the queen and **Much More Important** than him, Sidney couldn't help speaking his mind. He didn't think Elizabeth should marry the duke — and he told her so in a VERY long letter. (Well, words were his job. It's not surprising that he used a lot of them.)

The queen wasn't best pleased with Sidney's opinion of the duke and became **Very Cross** with him.

Sidney left court **Very Quickly Indeed**. And then wrote a lot of **Very Romantic Poetry** because he had so much spare time.

But by 1581 he was back at court. Two years later, he was knighted. The year after that, he was an MP. It was all looking good for Sir Philip Sidney...

... until Elizabeth sent him to the Netherlands to fight against Spain and his luck ran out. Sidney was shot in the leg, the wound became gangrenous and he died at the age of just 31.

But it was on his deathbed that the dashing, romantic hero became properly famous. While lying wounded, it's said that he gave his water bottle to another wounded soldier, saying, 'Thy necessity is yet greater than mine.'

Awww. So in the end, he was **Very Brave**.

Silt saved the *Mary Rose*

The *Mary Rose* was probably the most famous Tudor warship ever. Unfortunately, she was also the unluckiest. Because in 1545, just a short distance from the docks in Portsmouth where she was built, the *Mary Rose* sank during a sea battle.

So how exactly did silt — the gloopy mixture of grainy sand and water on the seabed — save Henry VIII's fabulous warship?

★ And the truth is...

Silt clearly didn't save the *Mary Rose* from sinking, but it DID do a pretty good job of preserving the warship — and everything that sank with it — for future generations.

When the 800-tonne timber vessel sank, silt swirled around it, settling everywhere, both inside and out. The *Mary Rose* was soon stuck so fast to the seabed that all Tudor salvage attempts failed. And when clay settled on top of the silt, a huge section of the ship was sealed tight, safe from further harm.

After the shipwreck was found in 1971, the Mary Rose Trust kicked off its rescue effort. It was a long and difficult job, but in 1982, the remains of the shipwreck were carefully lifted from the bottom of the sea at last. They now sit in the Mary Rose Museum in Portsmouth, UK. Go and see the shipwreck for yourself!

Verdict: _____ Sort of **TRUTH**

ZOUNDS!

The *Mary Rose* was a treasure trove of Tudor artefacts (AND Tudor facts) for the marine archaeologists who raised and restored her. And we're not talking a handful or a treasure-chest-full here. There were 19 THOUSAND priceless historical bits and bobs.

Here are just a few...

- Three-legged cauldron, just the right size for cooking a tasty meal for officers. (The other crew would have been served from a MUCH larger pot, because there were way more of them.)

- Bandages, pre-soaked with oil and resin that would harden when wrapped around fractured limbs. (That's old-fashioned plaster-of-Paris!)

- Wooden pomander on a rope. A Tudor sailor would stuff the hollow pomander with sweet-smelling stuff and then hold it near his nose so that he didn't notice the whiffiness all around!

- Porridge shovel for serving breakfast to the crew. (That's right. A shovel. The *Mary Rose* usually had about 400 crew on board, but in times of war, it could be as many as 700. That was a LOT of porridge eaters.)

- Nit comb. (Complete with real Tudor nits!)

- Tudor violin. (One of the oldest in the world)

- Divers also found swords, syringes, rat bones, thigh boots, mallets, guns, anchor cables, longbows, arrows, brass navigational dividers, pewter plates, beer tankards, book covers, cannonballs, peppercorns, plum stones, shoes, belts, cut-throat razors, dice and a coin featuring the image of Henry VIII himself!

One Tudor woman was given a seat at her own execution

Mary I wasn't the only Tudor monarch to burn heretics at the stake. Henry VIII did it too. Even though he'd fallen out with the Pope and the Roman Catholic Church, he didn't like members of his very own Church of England to hold extreme Protestant views either. And that's why Anne Askew — a poet and a Protestant — was sentenced to death in 1546.

But was she really given a seat to watch the whole thing?

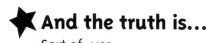

And the truth is...

Sort of, yes.

Anne Askew didn't just suffer an execution. In an attempt to get her to change her religious views, she'd already been tortured in the Tower of London, where she was stretched on a rack until her bones popped out of their sockets. (Yes, really.) And because she hadn't given in, she'd been sentenced to death. But poor Anne had been so horribly injured in the torture chamber, she couldn't walk to her own execution. She had to be carried to the stake on a chair instead.

Verdict:

People were allowed to treat their servants however they liked

In Tudor times, many, many people were employed as servants, especially the very poor. Henry VIII took 800 servants with him whenever he visited Hampton Court Palace! They were poorly paid, yet in return expected to be on call at any time — day or night. And if a servant upset their master, they could be beaten.

How AWFUL.

★ And the truth is...

That's not all. Sometimes, masters even KILLED their servants.

One Tudor nobleman chopped his cook's head with a cleaver so hard that the head fell in two parts, but he claimed that it was an accident and so was never brought to trial.

Henry VIII was one of the worst offenders. If anyone upset him, he punished them. And if anyone REALLY upset him, then he had them executed.

Yikes.

Verdict:  but only the very rich and powerful got away with it

A Tudor woman was once killed by a loaf of bread

Really? Loaves aren't usually prime suspects in murder mysteries...

★ And the truth is...

A certain Tudor woman, Elizabeth Bennet, was making bread on 29 January 1558. She went to the moat* to collect cabbage leaves** to put under the loaves she was baking, to prevent them from burning. The fence broke and she fell into the moat and drowned.

Crumbs! (Sorry.)

Verdict:

A moat is a kind of deep, water-filled trench that often surrounded castles or other fortified positions in Tudor times. Not really the sort of place you'd want to go for a dip...

**Cabbages grow best in damp soil with good drainage, just like the soil commonly found near moats.*

It's a popular belief that witches were burned at the stake. They had to be found guilty of witchcraft first, obviously. And in 1563, Queen Elizabeth I's government passed a law that made it a capital offence to cause the death of a person by witchcraft, which made it perfectly legal to hand out the death penalty. So, if the witch was found guilty of harming or killing someone, it was off to the bonfire with them.

Or was it...?

And the truth is...

Actually, a convicted witch's destination was usually the gallows. It was more common for witches to be hanged than burned alive.

The condemned person usually stood beneath the gallows, on the back of a horse-drawn cart. Once the rope was looped around their neck, the horse was led away and they were left to hang. The lack of a sudden drop often meant that the victim died slowly of strangulation. But if those operating the gallows were in a good mood, relatives were allowed to pull on the victim's legs to hasten the process.

Sometimes

but more often

Verdict:  TRUTH — BUSTED

You didn't have to be a witch to cast spells

In Tudor times, many people believed that witches possessed powers given to them by the devil. They were feared and shunned. (And hanged. And burned at the stake. See pages 38-39 for more on this.) So how could normal, non-magical people fight this evil?

⭐ And the truth is...

In a deeply religious world, many people thought that the forces of good and evil were pitted against each other. But they also thought that it was possible to prevent witches having power over them. And *Bald's Leechbook* was an old medical book featuring all sorts of weird and wonderful ways to fight back against evil... with yet more spells. Here are two of them:

Is **NASTY GOSSIP** doing your head in?
Don't worry!
Just eat a radish at night,
then fast the following day.
Then no gossip
can harm you.

Or do you suspect someone of **WITCHCRAFT**?
How do you keep yourself safe from
their **EVIL POWERS**?
No problem!

Simply make a potion from hops, vervain, garlic
and fennel. Place these in a vat under an altar,
sing nine masses over it, boil it in butter and
sheep's grease, add holy salt and strain the liquid
into a cloth. Rub this on yourself and you'll be
safe from the evil doings of witches!

Er, right.

but only if you're daft
enough to believe all this
witchcraft nonsense

Verdict: TRUTH

TUDOR TITBITS

I kid you not!

The last so-called witch to be burned at the stake was Janet Horne at Dornoch in Ross-shire in 1727. She had been accused of 'witching' her daughter to make her hands and feet grow into hooves, so that she could ride her like a horse. The daughter's hand was deformed, the accusers believed, because she had been 'shod by the devil'.

One easy way of finding out whether someone was a witch or not was by 'swimming the witch'. The accused was thrown into the village pond. Kersplosh! So how did they

work out if they were a witch or not? Simple.
The guilty floated and the innocent sank.
Now, how fair is that?

Another test was to weigh the accused against
the Bible. If the Bible was heavier, she was
clearly a witch.

only royal Tudors were allowed to wear purple

Anything goes, today. You can wear what you like. (Unless you have to wear a school uniform, obviously. Then, not so much.) The Tudors liked to dress up too, especially the rich ones, who could afford to wear fancy costumes, glittering with jewels. But were royals *really* the only people who could wear purple?

I say, do you think I could get away with lilac?

Sorry, the purple cloth is for royalty only.

⭐ And the truth is...

Yes, they were.

There were actual laws that defined what the different ranks of people at court could and couldn't wear. For example, only royalty were allowed to wear purple, while golden cloth was reserved for royalty and dukes. The laws were made to stop Tudors who'd made their own fortunes from showing off with costly clothes and goods.

Elizabeth I passed more sumptuary laws — as they were called — than any other Tudor monarch, particularly towards the end of her reign when they started to become more than a little bizarre. For example, cloaks were banned at court because it was thought that they made it harder for men to grab their swords to protect the queen. And for a time, it was even the law that you had to wear a hat in the queen's presence.

Verdict:  **TRUTH**

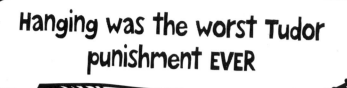

Hanging was the worst Tudor punishment EVER

Well, you'd think so, wouldn't you? Death by hanging could take a v-e-r-y long time, whereas beheading — if done properly — was over in a trice. So what could be worse than a slow strangulation on the end of a rope?

★ **And the truth is...**

Actually, those who were JUST hanged* got off lightly. Because if a person was found guilty of high treason, they faced a fate that was far, far worse...

They were HANGED, DRAWN and QUARTERED.

It's even more horrible than it sounds.

First, the victim was HANGED... but not totally. When they were very nearly dead, the convicted Tudor was taken down from the gallows and then DRAWN — or dragged — through the streets by a horse. Their insides were also DRAWN — or pulled — out and thrown onto a fire. (Some other bits were also chopped off. Yikes.) Then, they were BEHEADED. And then they were QUARTERED — their body was cut into four pieces. Finally, their head and other bits of their body were put on spikes somewhere everyone could see them. (London Bridge was a top spot.)

Verdict: **BUSTED**

Psst!

The good news for women found guilty of high treason was that they weren't hanged, drawn and quartered, because it was considered improper.

The bad news for women found guilty of high treason was that they were just burnt at the stake instead, which was quite a rubbish way to die too.

Psssssst!

* A person is hanged, not hung. Do correct anyone who gets it wrong, especially a grown up because I find they are the WORST offenders. Not that I've got a bee in my Tudor bonnet about it or anything.

John Stubbs thanked the queen for chopping his hand off

John Stubbs was a Puritan who had very strict Protestant beliefs. When, in 1579, Elizabeth I was wondering whether she should marry a Frenchman named the Duke of Anjou, Stubbs wrote a pamphlet in which he said that a wedding would be a very bad idea. He objected to the fact that Anjou was Catholic and worried that he might force the return of his faith to England. Besides, he argued, at the age of 46, Elizabeth was too old to have children. So there was no need for her to get married.

⭐ And the truth is...

There are no prizes for guessing that Elizabeth was FURIOUS.

In fact, she was so cross that she condemned both Stubbs and his printer to death by hanging. Luckily for the two men, the queen was persuaded to be more lenient – so she decided that they should have their right hands cut off with a mallet and a cleaver instead.

After his right hand was cut off, Stubbs removed his hat with his left, cried, 'God save the Queen!' and promptly fainted.

You've got to hand it to him.

Verdict: ⭐ TRUTH ⭐

The Tudors had their own Ice Age!

Oh, really?

An ice age is a long period of time during which the temperature of the Earth's surface and the air above it is much colder than usual. Ice sheets at the North and South Poles get bigger, making sea levels drop. Meanwhile, glaciers creep and grow.

Was it THAT cold during Tudor times? Did they freeze in their doublets and shiver in their hose?

★ And the truth is...

While the Tudors were in no danger from the woolly mammoths and sabre-toothed tigers that roamed Earth during the last ice age (which happened thousands of years ago), there's no question that it was really quite chilly when Henry VII and his descendants were on the throne.

In fact, the Little Ice Age — if you want to sound super clever, call it LIA for short — lasted from the 16th to the 19th centuries, so long after the Tudors were in power.

It wasn't a proper ice age. It simply wasn't cold enough for that. But it was so cold that London's River Thames froze over during many winters.

During the totally teeth-chattering winter of 1536, Henry VIII is said to have whizzed by sleigh along the Thames from the middle of London to Greenwich. In 1564, it was cold enough for Elizabeth I to stroll there too. Shortly after the queen died, Londoners finally cottoned on to the fact that this was a brand new — albeit temporary — piece of land where they could have fun. And in 1607, they held the first River Thames Frost Fair on the ice.*

Verdict:  but it wasn't a REALLY icy ice age

* Do not hold your own frost fair on a frozen river. Our winters are nowhere near as cold as they used to be, which makes it sillier and more dangerous than marrying Henry VIII.

Tudors didn't use forks

Ha ha!

So how DID a Tudor tackle massive meaty feasts? With just a knife?

⭐ And the truth is...

Actually, yes. And a spoon if they could get their hands on one, but these were shared, so it meant sharing everyone else's germs too. (Urgh.)

In fact, Tudor tables weren't laid with cutlery at all. Dinner guests usually carried their own knife — you never knew when you might need one — and this was used to cut AND to spear food. So it did the job of both a knife and a fork.

It wasn't until much, much later that forks were used at the dinner table.

Verdict:

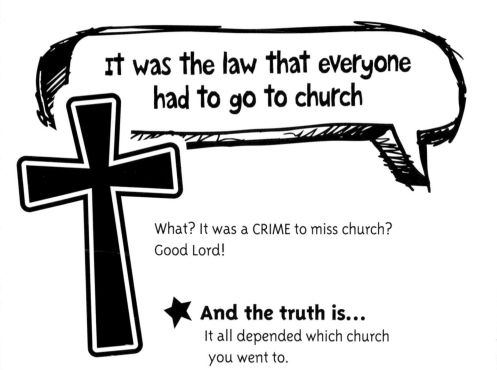

It was the law that everyone had to go to church

What? It was a CRIME to miss church? Good Lord!

⭐ And the truth is...
It all depended which church you went to.

Today, people can choose whether they want to go to church on Sunday morning, or not. But having a lie-in just wasn't an option in Tudor England. Everyone over the age of 14 HAD to go to church. A Protestant one. And those who didn't attend were fined.

Meanwhile, attendance at a Mass (a Roman Catholic service) was given a HUGE fine.

But the worst possible punishment was dished out for saying Mass, or arranging for it to be said, after Henry VIII changed the country's religion to the Church of England. That carried the death penalty.

Verdict:  TRUTH but only the right kind of church

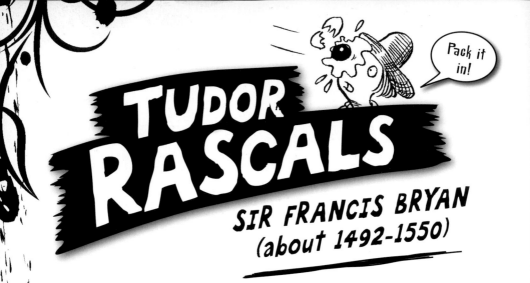

TUDOR RASCALS

SIR FRANCIS BRYAN
(about 1492-1550)

Francis was a courtier and a best mate of Henry VIII. This was either because he actually did love the same things as the king — jousting, hunting and eating — or maybe because he always made sure that he agreed with everything the king said. (Frankly, that was the best way to stay alive.)

In 1526, he lost an eye during a tournament and wore an eye patch forever after, which might have made him look a proper rascal, except no paintings of him survive so no one can check. And when the king sent Bryan to France, he teamed up with his brother-in-law, Nicholas Carew. Together they got up to all sorts of mischief. One of their most notorious escapades was riding through Paris in heavy disguise, throwing eggs at the locals.

Oh, ho ho ho.

But Bryan was ruthless when he needed to
be. Anne Boleyn was a cousin of his. (Many of the
nobility were cousins, but the term 'cousin' could apply
to very distant relations, as well as closer family members.)
And after bigging up Anne before her marriage to Henry
VIII, he didn't hesitate to turn on her when the king wanted
rid of her. For this charming behaviour, he earned himself a
nickname — the Vicar of Hell.

Luckily, Bryan had another cousin to fill the slot vacated by
Anne Boleyn — Jane Seymour, Henry's third wife.

But even though Sir Francis Bryan was a proper back-
stabbing rascal, sucking up to the king had
one major benefit — he didn't get his head
chopped off. Instead, he died suddenly
in Ireland of unknown causes.

That's enough! I mean, un oeuf!

Begging was a crime

In Tudor times, not everyone was able to afford ruffs and jewels and fancy clothes. In fact, most people weren't at all well off and a third of the population was officially poor. Vast armies of the very poorest tramped the countryside in search of food and work. Townspeople feared their arrival so much that they even wrote a nursery rhyme highlighting the problem:

'Hark, hark, the dogs do bark

The beggars are coming to town...'

Because there were no welfare benefits for the poor, surely their only choice was to beg?

And the truth is...

As ridiculous as it sounds, instead of rich Tudors helping the poorest members of their society to survive, they actually made it harder.

First, people needed a licence to beg, but these were only granted if they were old or ill. Then another law was introduced that made it illegal for people to leave their own town or village if they had no job. And here are some of the punishments dished out to the poor unfortunates who were caught...

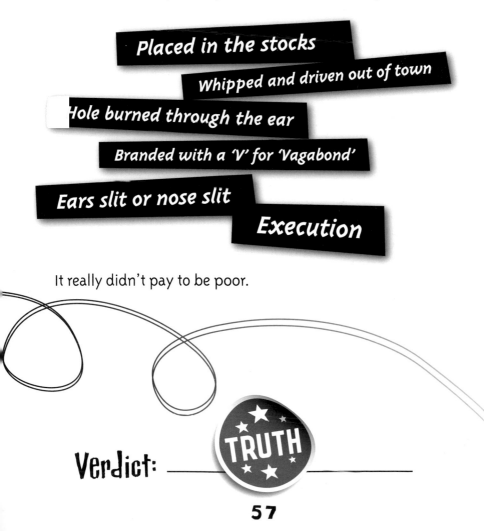

Placed in the stocks

Whipped and driven out of town

Hole burned through the ear

Branded with a 'V' for 'Vagabond'

Ears slit or nose slit

Execution

It really didn't pay to be poor.

Verdict: _____ TRUTH _____

Tudor ruffs were invented to catch dandruff

It makes total sense, doesn't it? The word 'ruff' is part of 'dand**ruff**'. And look at all those handy folds all around the ruff — perfect for catching Tudor flaky bits!

Does my head look big in this?

And the truth is...

Sadly, no.

The ruff, which became properly popular when Elizabeth I was on the throne, was actually the very latest Tudor fashion.

A ruff was a circular collar made of linen or lace that was stiffened and pleated, before being pinned in place. There were lots of different styles. Women either wore a totally circular ruff that went all the way round their neck or a ruff that left a v-shaped gap at the front. The fashion for men was to wear ruffs that were much higher at the back than at the front.

Ruffs were meant to make the wearer look good, not catch their dandruff.

Verdict: **BUSTED**

Drunkards were forced to wear a beer barrel

In the 16th century, there was one alehouse for every 200 people, which is a lot of alehouses. A huge amount of alcohol was being drunk, which could mean a lot of rowdiness afterwards. So how did the authorities deal with the situation? Did they REALLY make drunks wear beer barrels to punish them?

 And the truth is...

Not always. The drunk could also be locked in the stocks as punishment. But if they were a real nuisance, then they could be made to wear a beer barrel (with holes for arms and head, of course). And the bottom of the barrel would be removed so that they could walk around, making it easier for more people to jeer and throw stones and rotten food at them.

Verdict:  TRUTH (Sometimes)

Tudor children drank beer

And what was wrong with water and milk exactly? Both were freely available in Tudor times. There was absolutely NO need for children to be drunk.

Cheers!

★ And the truth is...

The thing was that in Tudor times, you REALLY didn't want to drink the water. It was so badly polluted — with sewage, dead animals, you name it — that anyone who sipped it risked becoming very ill indeed.

No one knew that boiling water killed any harmful germs. But by huge coincidence, the beer-making process involves boiling water, which gets rid of all the nasty bugs. This meant that beer was safe to drink.

Beer was brewed in different strengths and children would be given the weaker variety. Nevertheless, they might drink about 3 litres a week, while adults supped 10 litres. They also drank cider (made from apples) and perry (made from pears).

So why didn't children drink milk?

The problem was that milk wasn't pasteurised as it is today, to get rid of nasty germs. And there was no way of keeping it cool and fresh for long either.

ZOUNDS!

Elizabeth's courtiers drank an extraordinary amount of ale. In 1593, the royal household guzzled 600,000 gallons of the stuff. That's nearly 3 MILLION litres.

Verdict: ——— TRUTH ———

ZOUNDS!

The Tudors weren't keen on locking up wrongdoers, especially if they hadn't done anything REALLY bad, for the simple reason that they'd then need to employ someone to guard them. So a top Tudor punishment was to humiliate the wrongdoer instead. The stocks and the pillory were wood and metal contraptions that were clamped around either the person's feet (the stocks) or their head and hands (the pillory) and locked tight. The public were then free to hurl whatever they fancied — insults or cabbages, perhaps — at them.

FANCY TRYING OUT THE STOCKS FOR YOURSELF?

Simply commit one of these minor crimes and you too could be pelted with rotten tomatoes!

* Become a shopkeeper and cheat a customer!
* Bake bread and sell underweight loaves!
* Tamper with a butcher's scales to trick customers!

And if you're a horse trader, simply push garlic up a horse's hooter to make it appear more lively. You'll get a better price AND public humiliation in one easy step!

Torture was illegal

Rebellions, conspiracies and foreign invasion were all very real threats to a Tudor monarch's power. So naturally, they wanted to encourage people to spill secrets about any plots or plans that were designed to hurl them off the throne.

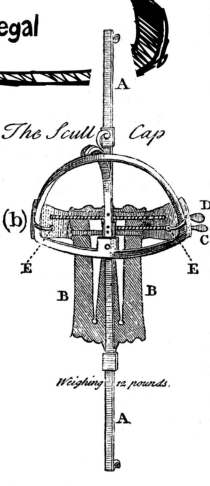

The Scull Cap

Weighing 12 pounds.

Except, there were rules about torture. It was illegal to torture anyone repeatedly. And it was definitely illegal to torture anyone to death.

So that's good.

★ And the truth is...

Unfortunately, Henry VIII and Elizabeth I especially were so worried about being overthrown that rules about torture were kind of ignored during their reigns.

Verdict:  not that anyone paid any attention to the law

Here are just a few of the terrible ways that Tudors were tortured to make them spill the beans...

THE RACK

This was a wooden frame with a roller at each end. The unlucky prisoner was strapped on — because you wouldn't want them wriggling about — and their wrists tied to one roller, while their ankles were tied to the other. The rollers were then turned in opposite directions. Ouch. The prisoner's body was s-t-r-e-t-c-h-e-d very, very slowly. This was so they had PLENTY of time to confess before their joints were dislocated. Owwwwww.

THE SCAVENGER'S DAUGHTER

This was the opposite of the rack. The prisoner wasn't stretched — they were SQUASHED instead. Poor Thomas Cottam, a Catholic priest, was both stretched AND squashed while in the Tower of London.

And then he was executed.

HANGING BY THE WRISTS

Richard Topcliffe was Elizabeth I's personal priest-hunter and torturer. And it was he who came up with the idea of tying the prisoner's hands together — usually behind the body — and hanging them by the wrists. But what if they were so tall that their feet touched the ground...? Ah. That wasn't a problem for the torturer. They simply dug away the ground from beneath the prisoner's feet so that they could swing freely. Sorted.

Tudor football players used jumpers for goalposts

Well, that would've been easier than building an actual goal. So, did they…?

⭐ And the truth is...

Of course not. Tudors didn't wear jumpers. Men wore breeches (short trousers), doublets (tight jackets) and cloaks — or tunics if they weren't that well off. Women wore dresses with frames underneath that were designed to make their skirts stick out. There wasn't a jumper in sight.

Tudors DID have goals, but these weren't 90–120 metres (or 100–130 yards) apart, as they are in today's soccer matches. They were ... wait for it ... 1.6 KILOMETRES (that's a mile) away from each other.

So how could the players even see each other, never mind play a game?!

Simple. There was no limit to the number of people on each side, so there were more than enough people on the pitch to pass the ball to. Sometimes, whole villages played each other.

Handball? Not a problem. If players wanted to pick the ball up and carry it, that was totally allowed.

And matches weren't restricted to 90 minutes either. Some went on for HOURS. Others, for DAYS. (Which is not surprising, considering the goalmouths were so far apart.)

But be warned. Football games could get quite violent and tactics included punching and even kicking. Some players DIED during matches.

Henry VIII tackled (geddit?!) the problem by banning football in 1540.

Verdict: —— BUSTED ——

A bear garden was a Tudor zoo

What could be pleasanter than seeing some nice, cuddly bears? Awwww.

⭐ And the truth is...

Unfortunately, the Tudors' attitude towards animals was a TINY bit different from ours. They were keen on totally bloodthirsty types of animal entertainment. One of their favourites was when specially trained dogs were let loose on bears and bulls in a wooden arena. But to make it even more of a spectacle — and safer for the audience — the bear or bull was fastened to a stake with an iron ring in the middle. The dogs were let loose on the tethered animal one by one, nipping and biting and generally worrying it until the angry bear or bull lashed out at them. And then there was a FIGHT.

The Bear Garden on the south side of the River Thames in London was also a theatre. It could house up to 1,000 spectators.

Verdict:  **BUSTED**

It was during the reign of Elizabeth I that women were finally allowed to appear on stage

Hurrah! Huzzah! And about time too.

★ And the truth is...

Sadly not.

It was still illegal for women and girls to perform in the theatre in Elizabethan times. Young boys played the part of women. It was only much later, during the 1660s, that an actress first appeared on the English stage.

Women weren't the only ones banned from acting in Tudor times. In 1572, strolling actors were barred too. It was feared that they might spread the plague. And besides, theatres were said to encourage drunkenness and thieving. Elizabeth, however, gave permission for four noblemen to start their own theatre companies and employ actors, thinking that these at least would be respectable.

Verdict:  **BUSTED**

Tennis was illegal

Real tennis — which is a little different from the lawn tennis that's played today — is one of the oldest of all racquet sports. Like lawn tennis, it was played over a net, but like the game of squash, players could bounce the ball off the walls too. (They could even score points by hitting the ball into one of three goals high up on the walls.) Tudor tennis racquets were wooden and the strings were made of sheep gut. (Urgh.) As for the leather tennis balls, they were filled with hair. (Ewww.)

Was it really banned? Why? What could be more harmless than a friendly game of tennis?

★ And the truth is...

The Tudor government decided that tennis was very harmful indeed. People were enjoying themselves playing tennis when they should have been working hard instead! They became so cross about it that a law was passed in 1512, banning a whole range of games. Dice, cards, bowls, skittles and, of course, tennis were all on the banned list. But the rules did not apply to the rich — they were allowed to carry on playing everything!

Verdict: **TRUTH** *if you weren't posh*

Pack it in!

TUDOR RASCALS

HENRY HOWARD, EARL OF SURREY (1516/17-47)

Psst! This doesn't mean that the Earl of Surrey was born on the twelfth stroke of New Year's Eve 1516. It's just that no one knows for sure the year in which he was born. Fancy that.

Surrey was a Tudor poet who became famous for being one of the very first people to write sonnets. (A sonnet was a type of poetry that the great playwright William Shakespeare made very famous indeed.) And he had many royal connections too. Surrey's ancestors included Edward I and Edward III, while two of Henry VIII's wives were his cousins — Anne Boleyn and Catherine Howard. Surrey, who apparently wasn't bothered about his relatives losing their heads, also tried to matchmake his sister Mary with the Tudor king, but she was having none of it. Mary told Surrey that she'd rather cut her own throat than wait for the king to do it. (Sensible woman.)

Then, in 1547, Surrey was arrested and tried for treason. His crime? He'd added the coat-of-arms of the old king Edward the Confessor to his own, which only the king had the right to do. However, many historians suspect that this was just a way of bringing down the powerful Howard family who, Henry was afraid, might be planning to steal his crown.

Surrey was found guilty — there's a surprise — and beheaded at the Tower of London on 19 January 1547. Hi father, the Duke of Norfolk, was supposed to follow Surrey to the chopping block, but he was saved by the death of Henry VIII himself on 28 January 1547. Phew.

Wee was used to flavour beer

In Tudor times, water was so badly polluted that it was little wonder beer was more popular. But there were no regulations covering the production of beer and brewers would add their own mysterious ingredients to give their beer a unique taste.

But was wee *really* one of those ingredients...?

Last orders!

That's what they ALL say...

★ And the truth is...

The quality of the ale varied massively. In 1521, the poet John Skelton saw that Elynour Rummynge, who ran *The Running Horse* pub in Leatherhead, Surrey used hens' poo to flavour her brews.

But there is no record of a brewer using pee.

(Phew.)

There were beer tasters, who tested the strength of the beers. (One of William Shakespeare's dad's many jobs was drinking beer!) But apart from tasting the beer, another method for testing the quality of brews was to don leather breeches, pour the ale on a bench and sit in it. If the trousers stuck to the bench, the ale was deemed to be off.

Verdict: **BUSTED**

Tudors didn't use toilet paper

Ewwwwww.

How totally GROSS.

So if Tudors didn't use toilet paper, what DID they use...?

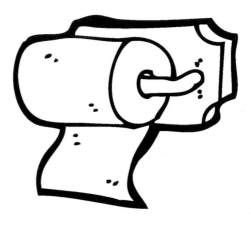

★ And the truth is...

It's not as bad as it sounds. Although the first toilet paper did appear in sixth-century China, the Tudors didn't use it. Instead, most used leaves or moss. Meanwhile, rich and royal Tudors wiped their bottoms with lovely, soft lambswool.

Apart from Henry VIII. That was the groom of the stool's, ahem, job.

Verdict: _____ TRUTH _____

Plague doctors soaked their clothes in vinegar

Er… right.

And why would they do that?

★ And the truth is…

Plague doctors had possibly the worst job in the world.* They treated people who were suffering from the bubonic plague and other highly infectious diseases. And because it was so easy to catch the plague — and then die from it VERY, VERY quickly and VERY, VERY nastily — the plague doctors did everything they could to avoid becoming ill themselves.

So, figuring that it was a good way of fighting the plague, they soaked their clothes in vinegar and then topped off their outfits with beaked masks, boots and gloves to make sure that the rest of their skin was covered up too.

Verdict:  TRUTH

Except maybe gong farmers. See page 86.

TUDOR TITBITS

I kid you not!

When the beautiful Christina of Milan was considered as a candidate for marriage to Henry VIII, she was said to have replied, 'If I had two heads, one should be at the King of England's disposal.'

Wise girl.

Can't remember what happened to which of Henry's queens? Don't worry! Simply recite this handy rhyme to remind yourself:

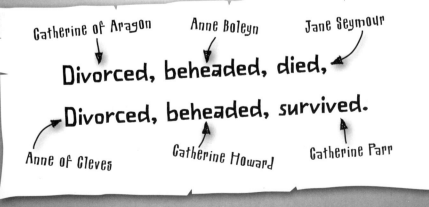

Catherine of Aragon   Anne Boleyn   Jane Seymour

Divorced, beheaded, died,
Divorced, beheaded, survived.

Anne of Cleves   Catherine Howard   Catherine Parr

Tudors thought that bleeding made you better

Really? Doesn't blood loss have a nasty habit of making the patient feel WORSE...?

★ And the truth is...

In Tudor times, bleeding was thought to be a definite aid to recovery. The Tudors believed that if a patient had too much blood inside them, it was bad for the body. And this led to the patient suffering from fevers. But if blood were let from the body, then the patient's illness would drain away with it.

The simplest method was to cut open a vein with a lancet — a sharp knife — and to let the blood flow into a bowl where the doctor could examine it. If that was too much to bear, then the doctor could use a blood-sucking worm called a leech instead.

Verdict:

P.S. Leeches have actually made a comeback! They are used in burns and reconstructive surgery units because of their excellent anti-clotting and blood-draining properties.

witchcraft could be good for you

Hang on a minute... What happened to witchcraft being BAD for you? What about those unfortunates who were hanged or burned at the stake because they were suspected of being witches?

Couldn't the Tudors make their minds up?

⭐ And the truth is...

Apparently not.

Both rich and poor asked witches for help with their problems. The Countess of Somerset, Sir Walter Raleigh and Lord Burghley were just a few top Tudors who used the services of witches. There are records of charms to cure people and animals, to help someone win at cards or to play the lute — a sort of Tudor guitar.

'A great many of us when we be in trouble, or sickness, we run hither and thither to witches, sorcerers, whom we call wise men and wise women... seeking aid and comfort at their hands,' said Bishop Latimer in 1552.

In short, there was good and bad witchcraft. And you were only found guilty if you had used your powers to bring about someone's death or illness. Strictly speaking, witchcraft was against the law after 1563, but that didn't stop it happening. When people were faced with difficulties they did not understand, they simply sought out someone who they thought might help, whether they were a witch or not.

Verdict: **TRUTH**

People threw their poo out of upstairs windows

And what's wrong with flushing it down the toilet exactly...?

★ And the truth is...

The Tudors didn't have flushing toilets; they had privies. And these were often VERY basic. Instead of a seat, there was just a slab of wood with a hole cut in it. And instead of a toilet bowl full of water and plumbing to flush everything away, there was a bowl.

It was against the law to throw waste into the street. But even so, some people DID do it... and faced the consequences.

One Londoner who poured poop down a drain was popped into one of his own pipes, which was filled up to his neck with filth and then publicly displayed in Golden Lane with a sign detailing his crime. Another group of Londoners was prosecuted when they built a privy over an alleyway.

Verdict:  but only a few got away with it

TUDOR RASCALS

Pack it in!

SIR FRANCIS DRAKE, THE PIRATE CAPTAIN (1540-96)

Was he a pirate? Or was he a sea captain?

Actually, Drake was both. It just depended whose side you were on.

Drake made his name as a daring sea captain who specialised in capturing Spanish treasure ships and taking home the loot to his queen. While Elizabeth I must have been delighted about this, the Spanish were not and they wanted the Tudor queen to punish him. But as Elizabeth I wasn't easy to push around, she ignored their pleas and made him Sir Francis Drake instead. (So he was a captain and a pirate AND a knight. Wow.)

As second-in-command of the English Fleet, Drake played a big part in defeating the Spanish Armada, which was sent to invade England in 1588. Next, he led campaigns against the vast, gold-rich possessions of Spain in the Americas. In one battle, he had a particularly lucky escape when a cannonball flew through the walls of his cabin!

When Drake died at the age of 55, he was buried at sea in a lead coffin. And as he'd requested, he was dressed in a full suit of armour too.

It's not surprising divers have never found him.

ZOUNDS!

Sir Francis Drake *is* über-famous for being a great Tudor explorer too. He sailed ALL AROUND THE WORLD. He wasn't the first to do so – that happened in 1522, when Ferdinand Magellan's Spanish crew did the honours – but Drake was the first to lead an entire expedition from start (in 1577) to finish (in 1580). And it was the first English circumnavigation of the globe too.

Are we there yet?

Tudor gong farmers had the worst job in the world

To work out whether this is the truth or totally busted, it helps to know what a gong farmer actually DID.

Are you ready? And, more importantly, are you eating? If so, STOP NOW.

Here goes...

Gong farmers collected people's poo and then spread it on fields or market gardens, because poo is not really the sort of thing you want piling up in your nice Tudor town where sewerage systems haven't been invented yet, but poo is a jolly good fertiliser for crops.

★ And the truth is...

Sorry, the prize for the worst job in the world actually goes to gong scourers, who were boys small enough to crawl along drains and clean them out. Ewwwww.

Verdict:  **BUSTED**

It's illegal to eat a swan

Rich Tudors loved pies made from game birds or water fowl, such as swan. For one swan recipe, the bird was often 'redressed' in its feathers and skin after the meat had been roasted.

But by eating swan, were the Tudors actually breaking the law?

And the truth is...

In 1576, during Elizabeth I's reign, a law called the 'Act for Swans' was passed, and is still in place today. The act decreed that all wild swans in England were the property of the Crown and that it was against the law to kill them.

But even though swans belonged to the monarch, that did not mean they couldn't be eaten... as long as the king or queen said it was OK.

Verdict:  unless the monarch gives you permission

P.S. A sauce called chaudon – made from vinegar, spices and swan's blood and giblets – is a superb accompaniment to roast swan. Apparently.

The Tudors baked pies with live birds inside

You've heard the nursery rhyme, right?

Sing a song of sixpence, a pocket full of rye

Four and twenty blackbirds baked in a pie.

When the pie was opened the birds began to sing,

Wasn't that a dainty dish to set before the king.

But did the Tudors actually DO this?

⭐ And the truth is...

They certainly did.

Sometimes, cooks who worked in wealthy nobles' households did indeed put live birds inside a pie. They were usually pigeons, but there's no reason why they couldn't have been blackbirds, as the nursery rhyme says. It was seen as a great joke to cut open a pie and release live birds, to the amusement of the dinner guests. The cook would be waiting with a proper cooked pie to bring in afterwards (thank heavens).

And here's how they did it...

'Bake the coffin of a great pie or pastry, in the bottom thereof make a hole as big as your fist. Bake the pie, and then open the hole at the bottom of the coffin. You shall put into the coffin as many small live birds as the empty coffin will hold. And this is to be done at such times as you send the pie to the table... where on uncovering or cutting up the lid of the great pie, all the birds will fly out, which is a delight and pleasure to the company.'

From Epulario 1598

What a shame they haven't invented Twitter yet. We could have tweeted about this!

Verdict: TRUTH

In Tudor times, the poor had a healthier diet than the rich

But the rich could afford to eat well, couldn't they?

How ridiculous to suggest that the poor ate more healthy food!

★ And the truth is...

Just because rich Tudors could afford to spend more on food, doesn't mean that they had a healthy diet. It was quite the opposite. They weren't too keen on vegetables, for example. But they LOVED meat. Here's what Elizabeth I's court once ate over a three-day period...

SHOPPING LIST

67 sheep

34 pigs

4 stags

176 pies

1,200 chickens

363 capons (a type of cockerel)

33 geese

6 turkeys

2,844 pigeons

2,500 eggs

195kg butter

1 cartload and 2 horseloads of oysters

Meanwhile, poorer Tudors ate vegetables, which were much cheaper. And vegetables were much better for them than, say, 34 pigs. Because an unrestricted diet of meat would have built up some nasty fatty deposits in the richer Tudors' arteries.

Verdict:

ZOUNDS!

Rich Tudors liked their food to be reeeeeally fabulous. Here are some of the more outlandish dishes they served up...

 The front of a chicken was sewed to the back of a pig before roasting. Snort! And, er, cluck.

 The Christmas pie didn't just contain turkey. There was pheasant, partridge, chicken and goose in there too.

 Forget about sage and onion stuffing. The magnificent multi-bird roast contained a bird within a bird within a bird — sometimes as many as 12 of them. Even more bizarrely, this came back into food fashion in the 21st century. You may even have eaten one, which means that you're practically royal.

 One of Henry VIII's favourites was roast bird gilded with REAL gold (which isn't cheap). Sometimes, this was mixed with saffron (which isn't cheap either) and butter (which is a bit more reasonable, and makes a good sauce).

> # It was a whipping boy's job to be punished

Well, you couldn't expect a prince to be punished, could you? He was FAR too important. What happened in Tudor times was that a whipping boy lived at court, just so that he could be beaten whenever the prince did something wrong.

WHAT?!

 And the truth is...

The clue's in the job title. Whipping boys were whipped.

It wasn't QUITE as bad as it sounds though. The whipping boy was usually one of the nobility — and one of the prince's friends — and he got to do lots of nice things at court too. But if the prince did anything wrong, then it was the whipping boy who received the punishment. The idea was that if the whipping boy was a friend of the prince, then the royal lad would hate to see someone suffering on his behalf and start behaving instead.

Verdict:  TRUTH

100%
SUCKER-PROOF

GUARANTEED!

Take a look at our other marvellously mythbusting titles...

Tip:
Turn over!